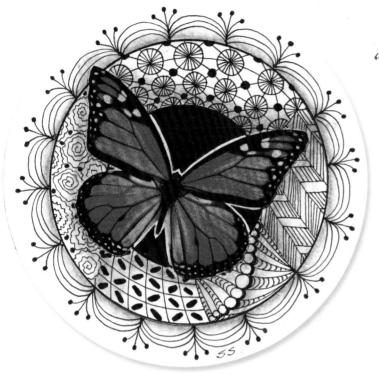

by Suzanne McNeill

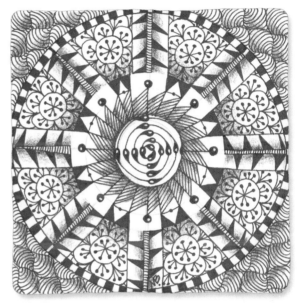

by Margaret Bremner

—Rick Roberts and Maria Thomas
zentangle.com

Zendalas

A Zendala is a form of mandala that is drawn using tangles to fill each section of a circle. These round gems are fascinating. In this book, talented Zentangle CZT artists generously share their secrets for creating basic circle designs, and how to add color, resist, layers, and more.

With Zentangle, the process is simple and relaxing (really!). Similar to handwriting, each person draws tangles in just a bit differen manner. Be inspired by the designs in this book and enjoy creating your own art.

Zen mandalas

For centuries, mandala circles have been used to connect the spirit with the divine, offering symbols found in nature as subjects of contemplation. Drawing a mandala helps one discover true inner self and balance. These special circles provide an opportunity to explore ancient teachings. Gently appreciate the uniqueness of your experience in the world of ten-thousand things as you create beautiful drawings that reflect your vision, and you will discover the infinite possibilities that spring from inner peace. When drawn on a Zentangle tile, each beautiful circle is called a 'Zendala'.

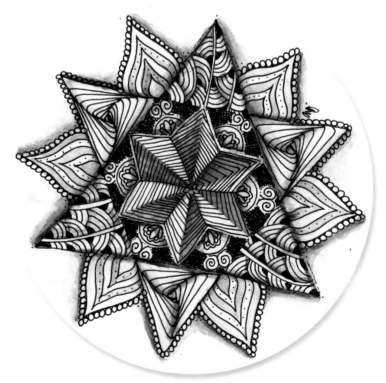

by Angie Vangalis

Classic Zentangle...

A very simple ritual is part of every classic Zentangle or Zendala drawing.

1. Use a pencil to form a border.
2. Draw guideline 'strings' with the pencil to divide the area into sections. The strings will not be erased but will disappear.
3. Use a black pen to draw Tangle patterns into each section formed by the 'string'.
4. Rotate the paper 'tile' as you fill each section with a pattern.

Starting a Zendala

1. Use a pencil to form a round border—use a circle template, compass, or lid. Add a dot in the center.
2. Now use the same circular shape to connect the center dot to the border, forming a partial circle.
3. Use the same circular shape two more times—always connecting to the center dot.
4. Use the same shape to divide the large sections into pleasing shapes.
5. Draw a smaller circle, to divide the large sections again.
6. Switch to a black pen and draw a tangle pattern in each section. When you cross a line, change the pattern. It is OK to leave some sections blank.

What you'll need to get started...

- a pencil
- a black permanent marker— a Pigma® MICRON 01 pigment ink pen by Sakura is suggested
- a Zentangle die-cut 'tile' is suggested—either a 4½" round 'tile' or a 3½" x 3½" square

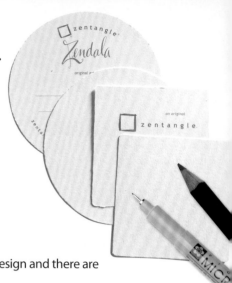

Each Tangle is a unique artistic design and there are hundreds of variations.

With Zentangle, no eraser is needed. Just as in life, we cannot erase events and mistakes. Instead, we must build upon them and make improvements from any event.

Life is a building process. All events and experiences are incorporated into our learning process and into life patterns.

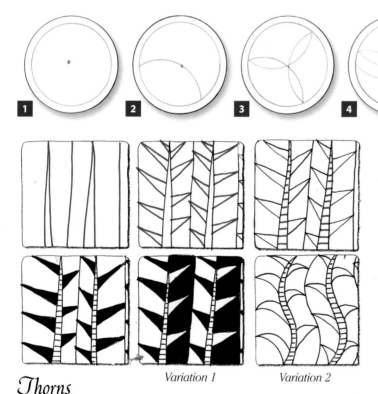

| 1 | 2 | 3 | 4 | 5 | 6 |

Thorns

1. Draw a line to divide the space into vertical rows. Draw a tall triangle section in the center of each vertical row.
2. Draw alternating horizontal triangles on each side of the tall sections to resemble 'thorns'.
3. Fill each tall section with horizontal lines.
4. Color the 'thorns' black.

Variation 1: Color alternating 'thorns' and background sections black.

Variation 2: Follow the steps above using wavy lines.

Variation 1   *Variation 2*

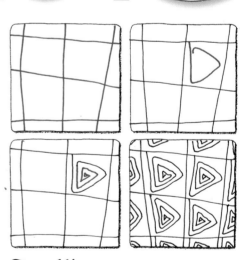

Time Warp

1. Draw a grid—curved lines are OK.
2. Draw a 'nesting' triangle in each square.
3. Draw each triangle in a continuous line until you reach the center with a tiny triangle.
4. Fill each section of the grid.

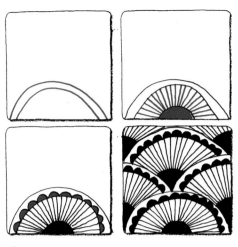
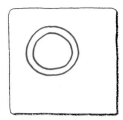
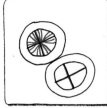

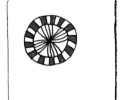
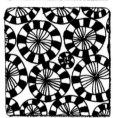

Citrus

1. Draw two large half-circles along one edge.
2. Draw a smaller half-circle in the center. Color the center black.
3. Draw radiating lines from the center to the border.
4. Draw small 'moon' shape humps in the border. Color the shapes black.

Florette

1. Draw two circles to form a border.
2. Draw a cross in the center. Draw curved lines radiating from each line to connect the center to the border.
3. Draw small sections in the border. Color alternate sections black.
4. Continue until the section is filled.

Puff Border

1. Draw a series of double 'moon' shape humps along the border.
2. Draw 3 lines between each 'moon' shape. Add a dot on the end of each line.

Practice a new tangle pattern and draw a new tile design every day.

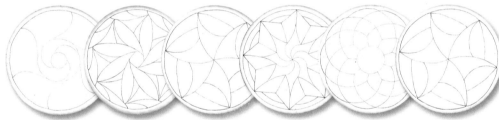

Pre-strung Tiles—Zendala tiles and square tiles are available from *zentangle.com* with pre-printed 'strings' so you can begin drawing tangles right away.

Shading Your Zentangle

Shading adds a touch of dimension.

Use the side of a pencil to gently color areas and details gray. Rub the pencil areas with a 'paper stump' to smudge, soften, and blend the gray shadows.

Note: Use shading sparingly. Be sure to leave white sections white.

A true 'Classic Zentangle' is created on a custom Zentangle die-cut 'tile' (a 4½" round or a 3½" x 3½" square) of archival print-making paper. Use a soft graphite pencil to create the string and Sakura's black 01 Pigma MICRON pen to create the tangles and to sign your Zentangle.

Helpful Basics:
- Remember to breathe.
- Hold your pen lightly.
- Be deliberate when making a stroke.
- Take your time drawing tangles.

Tips to Remember:
- Draw your strokes fluidly.
- Turn your tile from time to time.
- Stand back from your tile to view your work.
- There are no mistakes, only opportunities.
- It is OK to leave it and come back later.
- Enjoy the process.

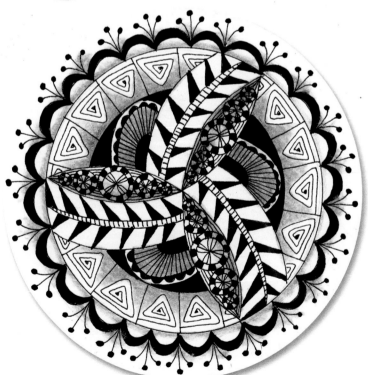

by Suzanne McNeill

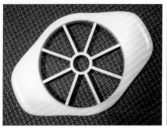 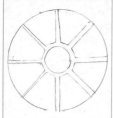 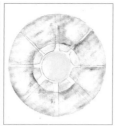 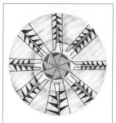 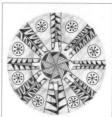 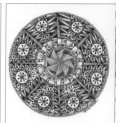

Colored Zendala: 1. Use an 'apple corer'. 2. Draw the rays in pencil. It will be a bit uneven. Don't worry about it. 3. Add color with Derwent Aquatone (or other) water-soluble pencils (yellow, deep pink, sky blue, purple). Use water and a small brush to blend the pencil into a wash. **Note:** Purple is stronger than blue and pink so use it sparingly.

4. Add tangles with MICRON 01 color pens. Try to co-ordinate the wash color with an ink color, and you will probably want to choose colors according to mandala segments. Use purple over purple areas. 5. Add filler tangles in green and orange. 6. Add shading with Prismacolor pencils in violet, fuchsia, and orange.

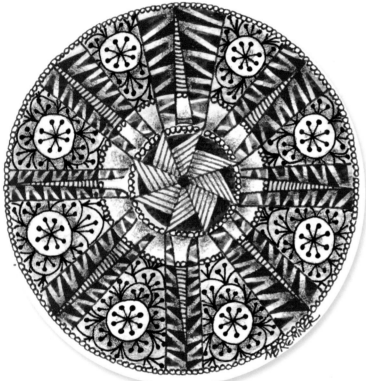

by Margaret Bremner

Margaret Bremner, CZT

Margaret tangles every day… it keeps her calm and sane. She has always loved detail and patterns and her discovery of Zentangle was an immediate click. Margaret is a prolific artist in acrylic, pen-and-ink, and mixed media. She is an active Zentangle teacher residing in Saskatoon, SK Canada.

email: margaret.bremner.artist@gmail.com
website: www.artistsincanada.com/bremner
blog: enthusiasticartist.blogspot.com

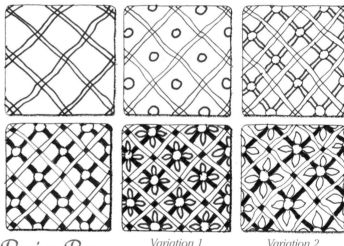

Persian Rug   *Variation 1*   *Variation 2*

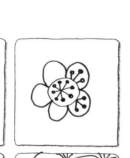

Blooms

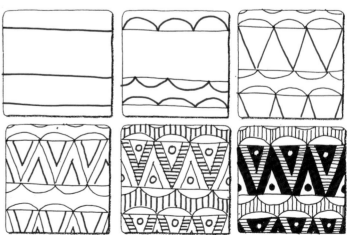

Cones   *Variation*

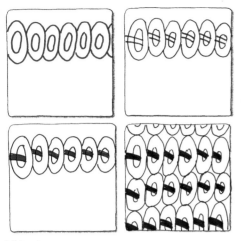

Washers

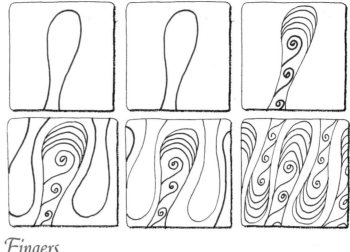

Fingers

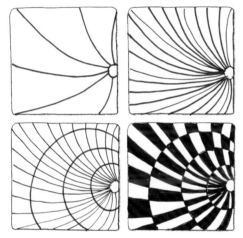

Radio Waves

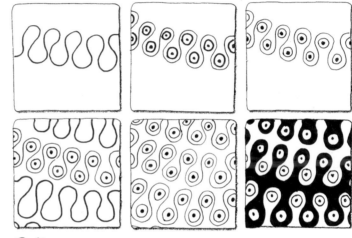

Culdesac

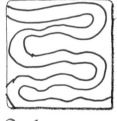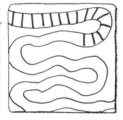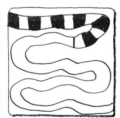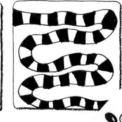

Snake

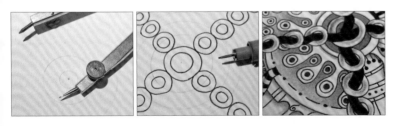

ZenDangle Circle: 1. Draw circles using a compass with a pencil tip. 2. Use a MICRON 01 black pen. Starting from the center, draw tangles radiating out. 3. Add tangles 'dangling' out from the center. Turn the tile as you work. Use a red MICRON to add spots of color. Shade areas behind some tangles.

INSPIRED BY 'ZENDANGLES' ART FROM THE BOOK ZENSPIRATIONS BY JOANNE FINK

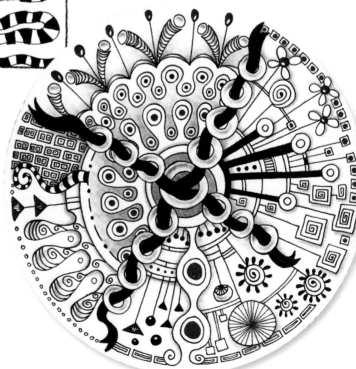

by Sandy Steen Bartholomew

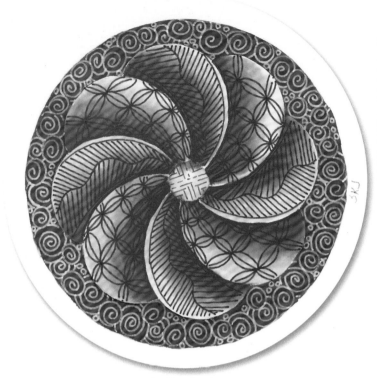

by Sue Jacobs

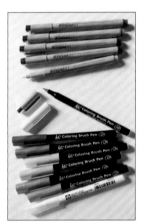

Watercolor Technique: Use water-based markers (Sakura KOI or Tombow) to shade areas of the donut with color. Use color Sakura MICRON 01 pens to draw tangles.

1. Apply color from a water-based marker to a piece of plastic. 2. Using a brush filled with water, dampen the entire section you are working on. 3. Pick up some color from the plastic with a damp brush and apply color to one side of a section. 4. Wipe out extra color and use the brush to spread color over the section—it will lighten as you go. 5. Let dry completely. Repeat these steps if you desire darker shading.

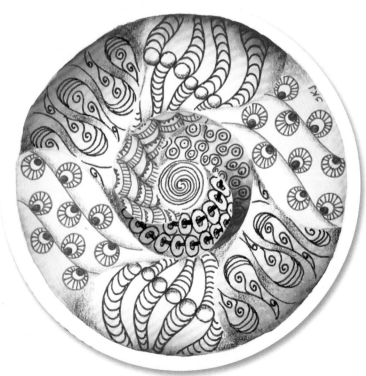

by Sue Jacobs

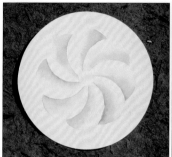 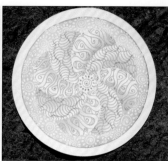

Spirals: Use water-based markers (Sakura or Tombow) to create the initial shading and to define the spirals. Use color MICRON pens to draw tangles. If desired, add extra shading at the end with a coordinating shade of a Prismacolor pencil.

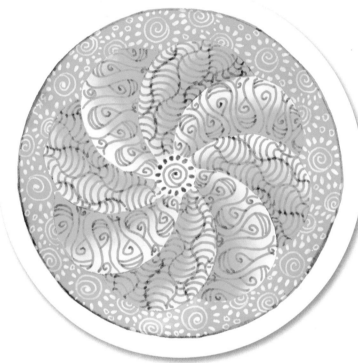

by Sue Jacobs

Sue Jacobs, CZT

Sue lets nature inspire her beautiful art. She is a talented artist and popular demonstrator. The pink and purple Zendala is an homage to the bright pink peonies in her garden. Her aqua Zendala is reminiscent of sky on a sunny day. Sue teaches Zentangle classes in the Chicago area of Illinois. You can see more of Sue's art on her blog.

email: sj60010@gmail.com
blog: suejacobs.blogspot.com

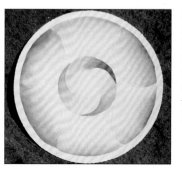

Donut: Use water-based markers (Sakura or Tombow) to create the initial shading and to define the sections. Use color MICRON pens to draw tangles. If desired, add extra shading at the end with a coordinating shade of a Prismacolor pencil.

by Sue Jacobs

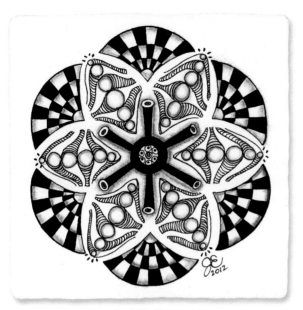

by Julie Evans

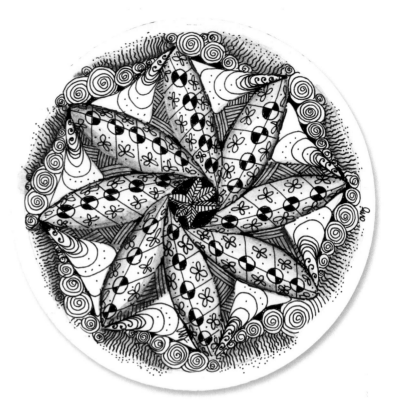

by Angie Vangalis

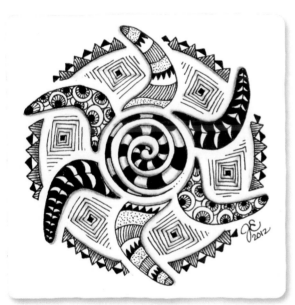

by Julie Evans

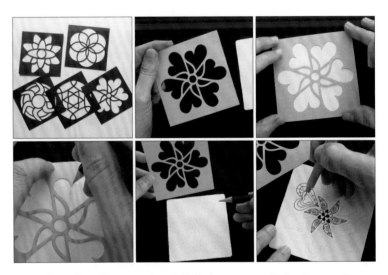

Use a Stencil: 1. Choose a stencil. 2. Gather a paper tile for the stencil. 3. Center the stencil on the tile. 4. Outline the sections with a pencil. 5. Remove the stencil. 6. Fill in the sections with tangles.

Julie Evans, CZT

Julie is a graphic artist and Zentangle teacher in Honomu, Hawaii. She is always looking for ways to enable her students to master the art of Zentangle. "I wanted a better way to introduce students to a round format, so with my graphic design background and the help of my Silhouette Cameo digital cutter, I developed… stencils for circles and Zendalas" (available at her Etsy store). These stencils create an outline that is begging to be filled with tangles.

email: julie@kalacreative.com
etsy store: KalaDalasStencils

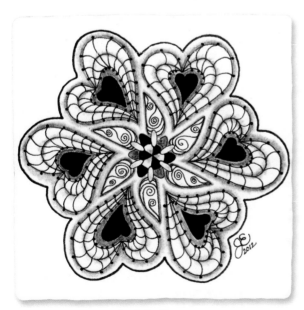

by Julie Evans

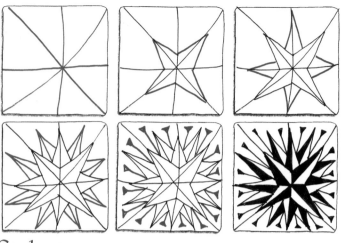

Starburst

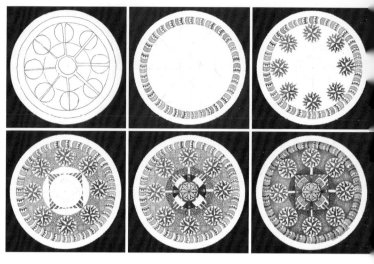

Circle Zendala: 1. Use a pencil and circle templates to draw sections for a design. 2. Use color MICRON 01 pens to fill the outer border with tangles. 3. Add a tangle in each circle. 4. Draw more tangles to fill the sections. 5. Fill in empty spaces with tangles. 6. Tint the background by shading with colored pencils.

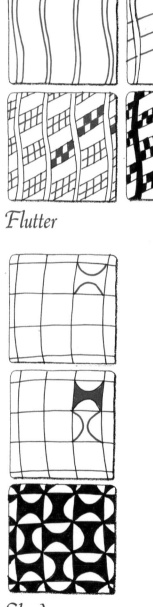

Flutter

Slender

by Margaret Bremner

This Zendala is enlarged, the actual size is 4½" diameter.

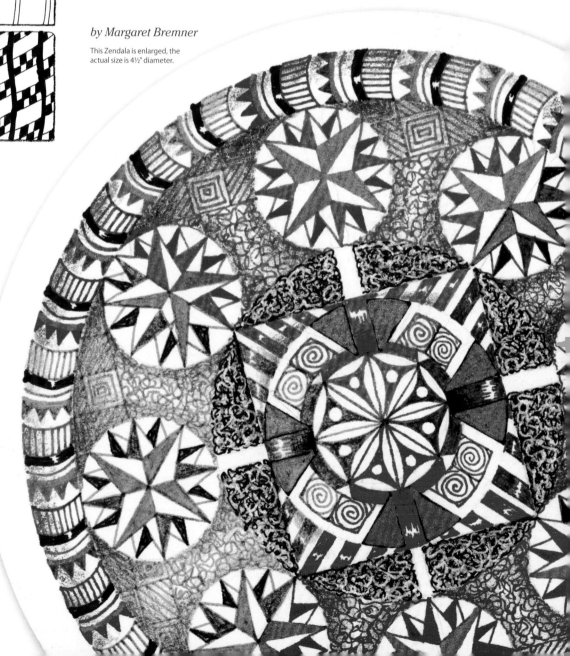

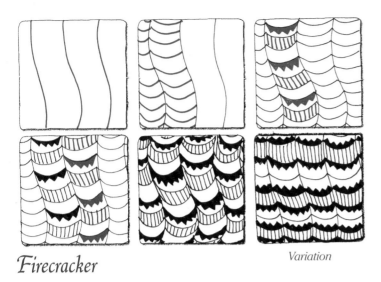

Firecracker

Variation

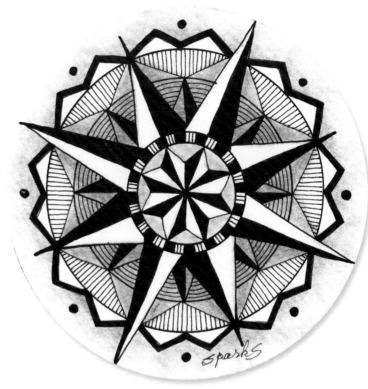

by Suzanne McNeill

Cracked Windows

Compass Rose

Elaborate compass rose drawings can be found on historic maps dating back to the 14th century. Sailors connected the points as a navigational aid.

These elaborate symbols divide the circle into thirty two directional points. In western culture, the points are simple bisections of the directions of the four winds—East, West, North, and South. Every apprentice seaman was required to master the naming of these points in a test known as 'boxing the compass'.

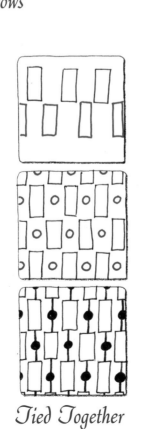

Tied Together

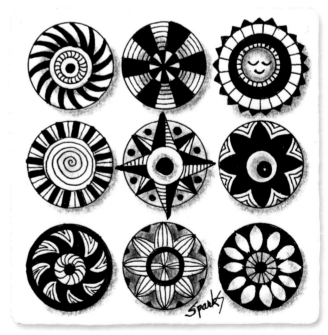

by Suzanne McNeill

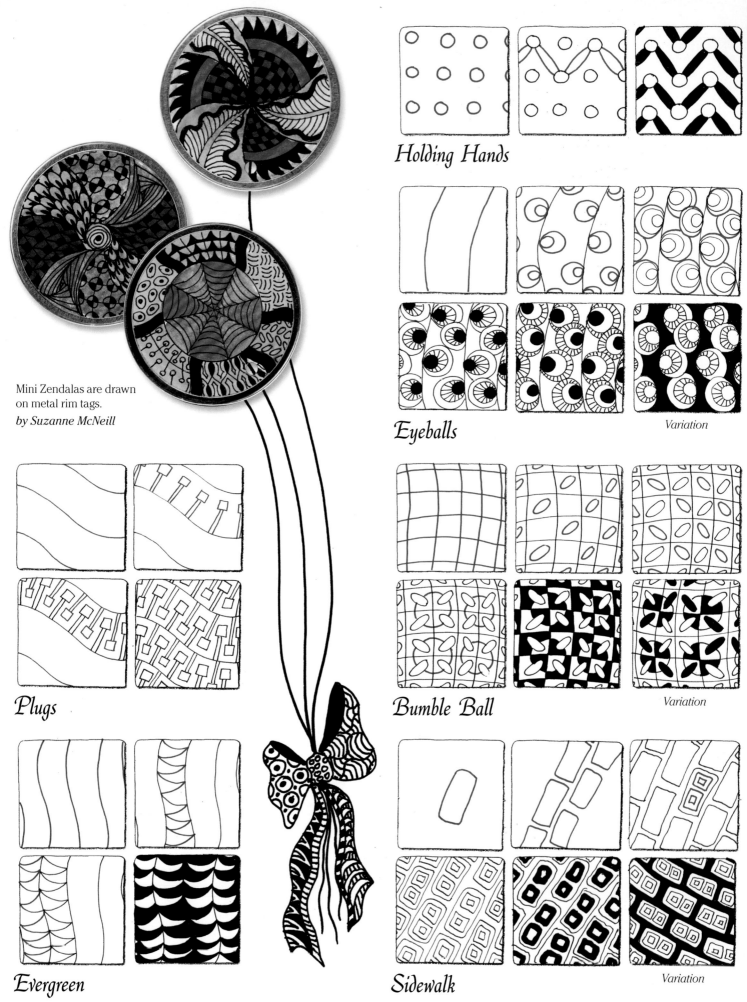

Mini Zendalas are drawn
on metal rim tags.
by Suzanne McNeill

Holding Hands

Eyeballs   *Variation*

Plugs

Bumble Ball   *Variation*

Evergreen

Sidewalk   *Variation*

Use a Resist: 1. Use a GellyRoll Glaze pen to draw tangles on a pre-strung Zendala tile. Let it dry over night. 2. Fill each section with watercolor paints (I love Yarka brand). 3. Let each section dry. Fill all sections with color. 4. Use Prismacolor pencils to add shading to the color areas.

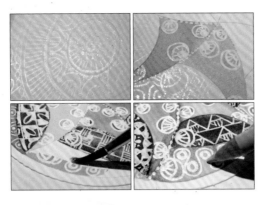

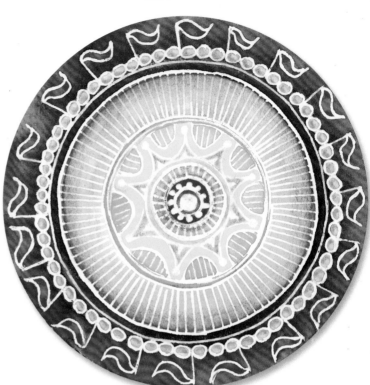

by Sandy Steen Bartholomew

Sandy Steen Bartholomew, CZT

Sandy is an author, illustrator, mixed-media artist, and Zentangle teacher from Warner, NH (Concord area). Her amazing tangle artistry is showcased in her books—'Totally Tangled', 'Yoga for the Brain', 'Tangled Fashionista' and in decks of 'Tangled Cards'.

email: beezink@tds.net
website: www.beezinkstudio.com

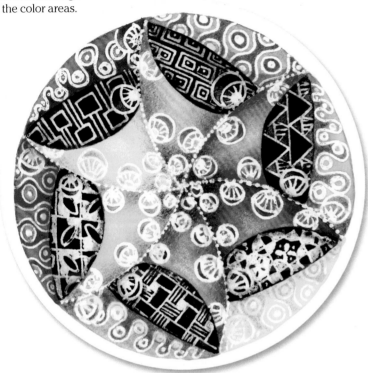

by Sandy Steen Bartholomew

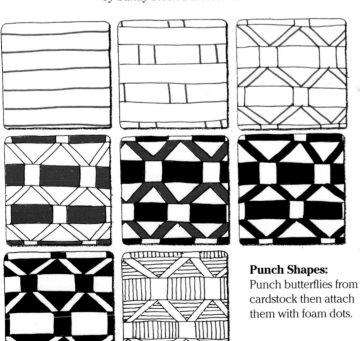

Variation 1   *Variation 2*

Punch Shapes: Punch butterflies from cardstock then attach them with foam dots.

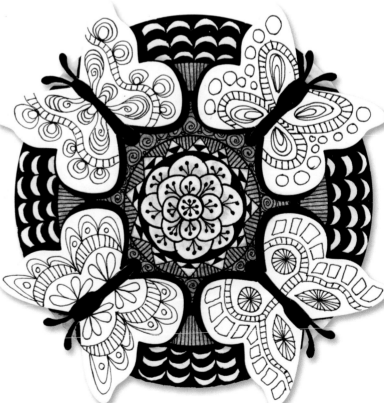

Tessera

by Suzanne McNeill

Angie Vangalis, CZT

Angie is a talented artist, calligrapher, photographer, and teacher of a creative Zentangle class almost every week. She is well known for her creative use of materials for tangling. Angie is also director of Texas Lettering Arts and encourages creativity through visits from guest artists.

email: angie@avgraphics.net

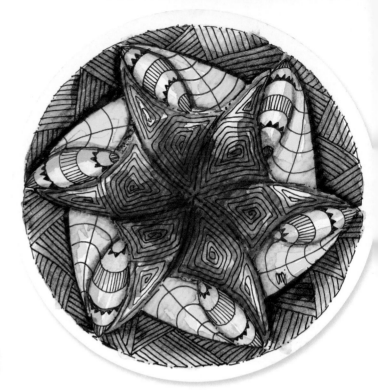

by Angie Vangalis

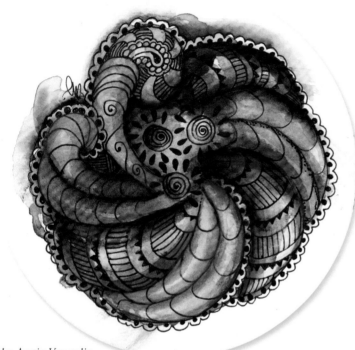

by Angie Vangalis

How to Watercolor

Technique 1: Dampen your brush then dip it in a color (add a drop of water to each color before you begin). Next brush color onto the design, section by section.

Technique 2: Make a 'puddle' of water, then add colors drop by drop. While it is still wet, tilt the tile to encourage the colors to run together in the puddle.

Draw tangles with a black MICRON 01 pen and let dry overnight.

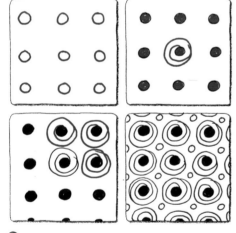

Spotty

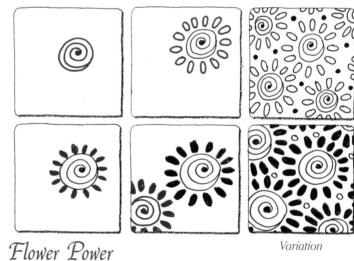

Flower Power

Variation

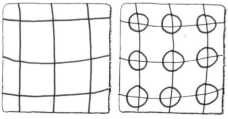

Grandma's Quilt

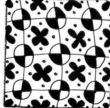

Variation

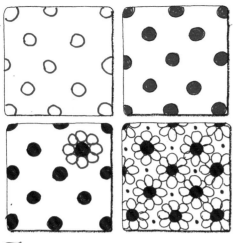

Flowers

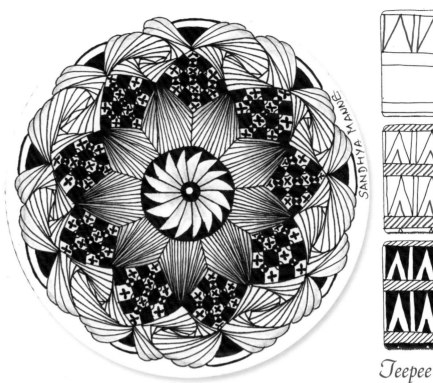

by Sandhya Manne

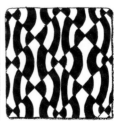

Teepee

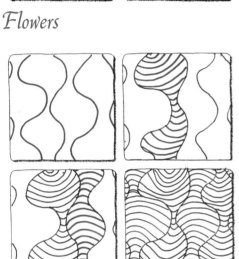

Cuddles

Sandhya Manne, CZT

Sandhya is an Indian artist living in the USA. Though mostly self taught she was fortunate to train under some successful artists during her travels around the world. Her works are abstract interpretations of the contemplative aspects from the cultures of India. They reflect peace, joy, and spirituality. She regularly exhibits in the Dallas-Fort Worth area and her works are in private collections in Canada, the USA and India. She offers Zentangle workshops and classes in Mckinney, Richardson, and Dallas. TX.

email: sandhyamannestudio@gmail.com
website: www.sandhyamanne.com
blog: www.zentempletangles.com

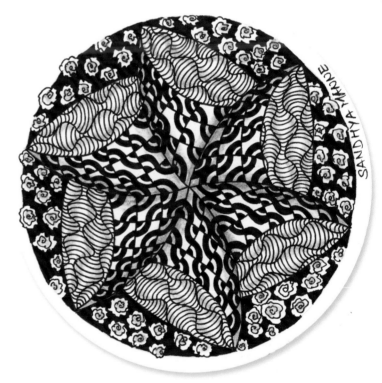

by Sandhya Manne

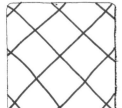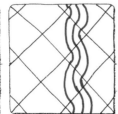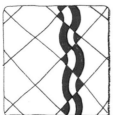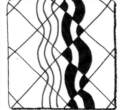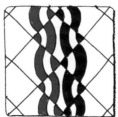

Fog Horn

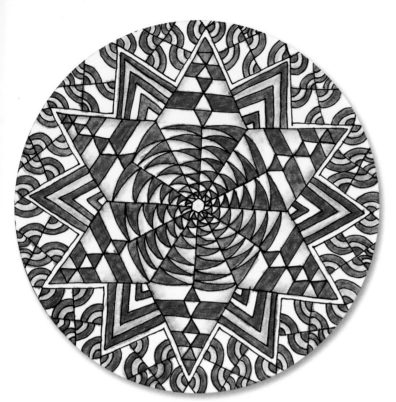

by Sandhya Manne

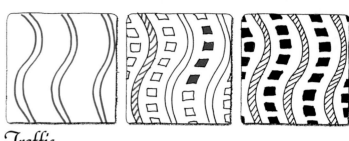

Traffic

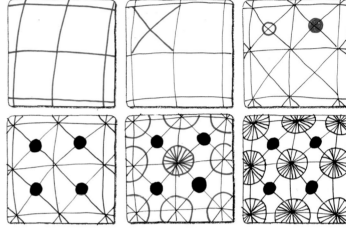

Parasols

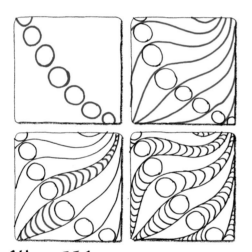

Worm Holes

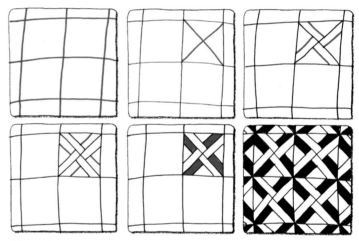

Depth

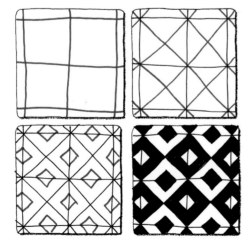

Parquet

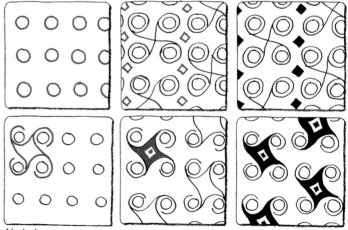

Variation

Sprockets

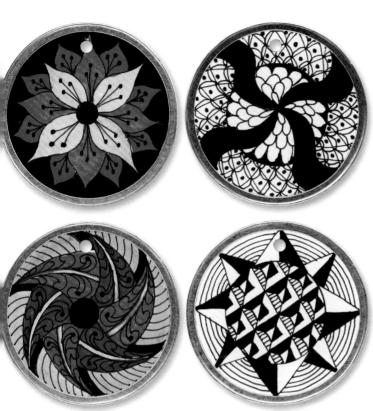

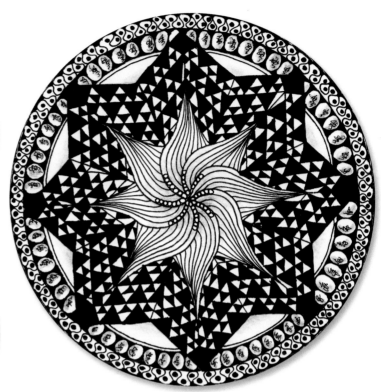

by Sandhya Manne

Mini Zendalas: These beautiful little Zendalas are drawn on 2¼" metal rim tags. it is easy to hang each one from a necklace string.

by Suzanne McNeill

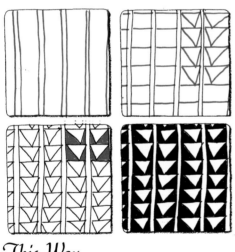

This Way

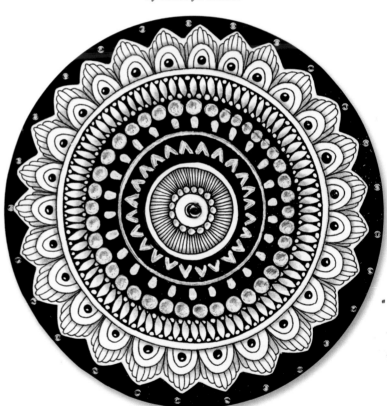

by Sandy Steen Bartholomew

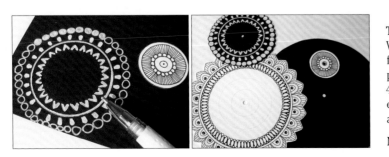

The Spinner Zendala is Sandy's favorite. It is layered and it can spin. Why? Why not!—1. Draw tangles on black cardstock with a white gel pen from Ranger. Draw on white cardstock with a MICRON 01 black pen. 2. Cut or punch four circles (2¾" and 4¾" black circles, 1¼" and 4½" white circles). Punch a hole in the center of each circle. Trim the edges of the 4½" circle. Layer and attach all the circles together with a brad. Add Stampendous Dot Sparklers stickers along the edges.

Note: These tangles are based on traditional Indian Mehndi patterns.

40 Fun Tangle Patterns from Zentangle® 7

Thorns
page 4

Time Warp
page 4

Florette
page 5

Citrus
page 5

Puff Border
page 5

Blooms
page 6

Persian Rug
page 6

Cones
page 6

Washers
page 7

Radio Waves
page 7

Snake
page 7

Fingers
page 7

Culdesac
page 7

Starburst
page 10

Flutter
page 10

Slender
page 10

Firecracker
page 11

Cracked Windows
page 11

Tied Together
page 11

Plugs
page 12

Evergreen
page 12

Holding Hands
page 12

Eyeballs
page 12

Bumble Ball
page 12

Sidewalk
page 12

Tessera
page 13

Spotty
page 14

Flower Power
page 14

Grandma's Quilt
page 14

Flowers
page 15

Cuddles
page 15

Teepee
page 15

Fog Horn
page 15

Worm Holes
page 16

Parquet
page 16

Traffic
page 16

Parasols
page 16

Depth
page 16

Sprockets
page 16

This Way
page 17

Suzanne McNeill

Suzanne is often known as "the Trendsetter" of arts and crafts. Dedicated to hands-on creativity, she constantly tests, experiments, and invents something new and fun.

Suzanne has been the woman behind **Design Originals**, a publishing company dedicated to all things fun and creative. She is a designer, artist, columnist, TV personality, publisher, art instructor, author, and lover of everything hands-on. Visit her blog to see to see events, books, and a 'Zentangle of the Week'. She also shares her techniques and ideas in youtube demos.

email: *suzannebmcneill@hotmail.com*
website: *sparksstudio.snappages.com*
blog: *blog.suzannemcneill.com*

ZENTANGLE®
You'll find wonderful resources, a list of certified teachers and workshops from around the world, a fabulous gallery of inspiring projects, kits, supplies, ATCs, prestrung tiles, Zendalas, and tiles.

ZENTANGLE
www.zentangle.com

SUPPLIERS
Most stores carry an excellent assortment of supplies. If you need something special, ask your local store to contact the following companies:

MICRON and GLAZE PENS, COLOR MARKERS
SAKURA, *www.sakuraofamerica.com*

CIRCLE STENCILS
KALA CREATIVE, *julie@kalacreative.com*

WATERCOLOR PAINTS
SAKURA, *www.sakuraofamerica.com*
YARKA

WATERCOLOR PENCILS
DERWENT
PRISMACOLOR

METAL RIM TAGS
AVERY, *averydennison.com*